Contra Costa Child Care Council
1035 Detroit Ave., Ste. 200
Concord, CA 94518

Good Going!

Contra Costa Child Care Council
1035 Detroit Ave., Ste. 200
Concord, CA 94518

Also by Gretchen Kinnell for the Child Care Council of Onondaga County, Inc.

No Biting: Policy and Practice for Toddler Programs

Good Going!

Successful Potty Training for Children in Child Care

Gretchen Kinnell
for the Child Care Council
of Onondaga County, Inc.

Redleaf Press
St. Paul, Minnesota
www.redleafpress.org

Published by Redleaf Press
a division of Resources for Child Caring
10 Yorkton Court
St. Paul, MN 55117
Visit us online at www.redleafpress.org.

This book is typeset in Stone Serif.
Cover designed by Laurie Ingram-Duren
Cover photograph © Stefanie Felix

Redleaf Press books are available at a special discount when purchased in bulk (1,000 or more copies) for special premiums and sales promotions. For details, contact the sales manager at 800-423-8309.

Library of Congress Cataloging-in-Publication Data
Kinnell, Gretchen, 1950–
  Good going! : successful potty training for children in child care / Gretchen Kinnell for the Child Care Council of Onandaga County, Inc.
    p. cm.
  ISBN 1-929610-46-7
  1. Toilet training. 2. Day care centers. I. Child Care Council of Onondaga County. II. Title.
  HQ770.5.K56 2004
  649'.62—dc22
                                                    2004002092

Manufactured in the United States of America
11 10 09 08 07 06 05 04   1 2 3 4 5 6 7 8

Acknowledgments

I would like to acknowledge the commitment of the child care centers and their head teachers and administrators who served on the original task force. Special thanks to the center directors who worked to arrange for their staff members to attend the task force meetings over the course of several months.

I would also like to recognize and thank Carol Eisenberg, Certified Pediatric Nurse Practitioner, for sharing her expertise and experience concerning medical issues associated with toilet learning. She is affiliated with Health Services Association in Syracuse, New York, and worked with the original task force.

I would like to recognize the staff of the Child Care Council of Onondaga County for their role in helping to address this issue and their encouragement in producing this book. I am especially grateful to Desalyn De-Souza, our Infant-Toddler Specialist, for her research into toilet training.

I want to acknowledge the past and present members of our board of directors for their vision and support. Deborah Holler, past Board President, was the first person to suggest that we put our good work on important issues into print and "write the book on it." And Peggy Liuzzi, our Executive Director, was the person who said, "Go ahead."

I would also like to thank Kathy Kolb at Redleaf Press for her advice and work turning a raw manuscript into a finished resource book. I am very grateful to Beth Wallace whose work as the Redleaf editor for my first book, *No Biting*, helped so much not only with that book, but also served as a guide to organizing *Good Going!*

Finally, I must thank my family for their support, patience, and great humor during the writing of this book.

Contents

Introduction

At first look it may seem that there are plenty of books on potty training and absolutely no need for yet another one. Parents of toddlers have a huge array of books on potty training to choose from that all approach toilet training as a home-based activity overseen by parents. Looking closer at the lives of toddlers, however, we see that not all of them are at home with a parent during the day. Many of them are in child care settings, and parents and caregivers alike need specific information on helping children learn this important skill when they are going back and forth between home and child care.

This is what we found at the Child Care Council of Onondaga County in Syracuse, New York. We receive many calls, from programs and parents, about potty training in child care, numbering second only to calls about biting. Administrators are frustrated by the demands of parents, parents are frustrated by the practices of the programs, caregivers are frustrated by inconsistent parent behavior, and toddlers are just plain frustrated!

Both parents and programs asked us to send them written information and resources they could use to make potty training go more smoothly for their toddlers. We found many books and articles on potty training in general, but none that addressed the unique issues arising when children are potty trained in two different places by two different sets of people. The differences between the two settings, we felt, were at the heart of many of the issues we heard about.

When toddlers are home all the time and are being potty trained there, parents can and do use many different methods. The home situation is basically one toddler, one place, one method. In group child care, there may be two, three, even ten toddlers who are all being potty trained. Child care programs may have two, three, even ten different suggested methods from parents about how to potty train their children. Experienced child care providers know that working with parents is extremely important. They also know, however, that it is not possible to have multiple potty training methods going on at the same time in one room. Even the most flexible child care provider would not be able to carry out a plan calling for several different potty training methods at the same time. The situation in group care really does have to be several toddlers, one method. The question then is which method? Certainly some will not work in group care. One that comes to mind right away is the "let-'em-run-around-naked-so-they'll-notice-they're-peeing" method. You don't even have to be a toddler caregiver to cringe at the thought of two, three, or ten naked toddlers running around, chased by caregivers pointing out streams of urine. Another one that comes to mind is the "sit-'em-on-the-potty-and-entertain-'em-until-they-urinate" method. In group care, this gives a whole new meaning to the term "circle time."

It quickly becomes clear that for potty training to be successful in group care we need a method that is carefully thought out, appropriate for toddlers, and appropriate for group care. Developing such a method, however, is only part of what we need to do. We must also realize that the children in our care are trying to learn, both at the same time, to use the potty at our programs and in their own homes. Therefore, we need to involve parents in the process so children will have enough consistency to be successful. How would this work? What would it look like?

The Child Care Council of Onondaga County's Toilet Learning Task Force

In 1994 we asked twenty-five experienced toddler caregivers to form a task force to focus on potty training in group care. We called our group the Toilet Learning Task Force. As the task force examined issues, it became apparent that developing a partnership between parents and caregivers was the key to success. We also realized that even within our own small group there was no consistent understanding or thinking about potty training. This was confirmed by administrators, caregivers, and parents we spoke with. Some administrators had thought about potty training and had procedures in place. Others only thought of potty training as a requirement for moving up to the next room. Some caregivers used a child-centered approach to potty training with the toddlers in their rooms. Others handled the whole process themselves based on whatever worked for them. Some parents based their understanding on what their own parents told them. (Mothers-in-law seemed especially powerful forces here!) Others relied on the latest potty training books or their pediatrician for information.

The task force addressed these issues by creating a booklet called, "Toilet Learning in Group Care: A Resource for Child Care Programs and Parents," with information, suggestions, and tips on potty training and on developing a partnership between parents and caregivers. In the subsequent years the Child Care Council continued to work with both parents and programs on potty training. We wrote articles, gave interviews to our local newspaper, and offered seminars on potty training in group care for both parents and programs. We made one small change in our approach and discovered one big change in an issue related to potty training.

Here is the small change. We called our original group the Toilet Learning Task Force. We deliberately wanted to avoid the word *training* and to stress the word *learning*. In the introduction to the booklet developed by that task force we stated

We want to acknowledge that this really is a learning process for children rather than something they are "trained" to do. Although at first "toilet learning" may seem awkward, it stresses learning and helps us give the process the serious consideration it deserves.

As we continued to work with both parents and child care programs we found that *potty training* and *toilet training* are the terms almost everyone uses to refer to this process. We also found it was possible to talk about the learning aspect of the skill and all the developmentally appropriate approaches and practices from the original resource even if we called the process *potty training*. It is important that both parents and caregivers feel comfortable talking with us about issues and problems so that they will have confidence in our information and with our suggestions. So we now use a variety of terms including *learning to use the toilet, potty training,* and *toilet training.*

The big change we discovered concerns parent-pressure for children to be potty trained. Members of the original task force worked with parents who consistently wanted their children potty trained at very young ages without regard to how ready the children were. This is still an issue, and we still hear from caregivers when parents ask them to potty train a child because "she just turned one, you know." More and more, however, we started hearing from caregivers that some parents weren't interested in having their children start potty training even though all indications showed they were ready. These parents often said, "I don't want to put any pressure on him. When he's ready, he'll just go." Other parents would say, "You know, it's just easier to keep her in diapers." The section on readiness (chapter 1) addresses both issues.

Developing a Perspective on Potty Training

Both in the work of the original task force and in our work at the Council since then, we found that there isn't even agreement among adults about what potty training involves and—more importantly—when a child is considered potty trained. Many toddler caregivers have had parents announce that their child is already potty trained. Then they go on to tell the caregiver what needs to be done for their "completely potty trained toddler."

> Just keep watching his face and notice when he looks like he has to go. Then take him to the potty and get him ready—you know, do his clothes because he can't undo the buckles or zip the zipper or snap the snap. You should stay with him for about five minutes. When he pees or poops, jump up and down, clap your hands and say, 'Whee! Whee! Did you ever pee!' or 'Whoop! Whoop! Did you ever poop!' You'll have to wipe him because he just really can't do that well enough to be

clean. Then just help him get dressed again and wash his hands. I usually try to take him to the potty about once an hour.

This example is, of course, exaggerated, but many toddler caregivers will recognize bits and pieces of it. The issue here is that the parents may truly consider the child potty trained because he urinates and has bowel movements in the potty. The caregiver, on the other hand, doesn't consider this child potty trained because an adult has to take charge of so much of the process. If we're going to talk about potty training in group care, we need to be clear about what we mean.

This calls for more than a definition of potty training. We need a way of looking at potty training that will guide what we do with children and with parents. The original task force developed a perspective on potty training, and we have expanded it over the past several years. The perspective has two main points:

- Potty training is a process that helps children master toileting as a self-help skill.
- When children are in group care, parents and caregivers must work together so the children can be comfortable, confident, and successful while they learn toileting skills.

This perspective is useful because it provides a framework and a direction for our work with children and parents. When we think of potty training as a process, we don't expect a child to be completely potty trained overnight. We realize that for most children this is a gradual process. So we expect it to take some time, and we look for incremental mastery. Our perspective also guides our instruction and interaction with children. We want to be moving children in the direction of being able to do the following for themselves:

- Realize they need to use the potty without anyone reminding them
- Take themselves to the potty
- Undress enough to use the potty
- Urinate and have bowel movements in the potty
- Wipe themselves
- Pull up their pants
- Flush the toilet
- Wash their hands

We can use this perspective to address many issues related to potty training. A good example is an often-asked question about wiping. Many adults want children to learn to wipe themselves, but worry that either they won't wipe well enough for good hygiene or that their efforts at wiping will end up being rather like smearing. Our perspective helps us look at wiping as a step in the process, which then becomes a self-help skill when mastered. It points us away from trying to have a one-word answer to the question of who should wipe, and directs us instead to figure out how we can create a process so eventually the child will be able to wipe herself well enough. We now suggest that adults and toddlers take turns wiping: the adult takes the first two turns and then trades off with the child. We also suggest that caregivers help children learn how to tell when they are clean enough by looking at the toilet paper they just used to wipe themselves.

This perspective also helps to clarify our role in the toilet training process. If we accept that children are learning to use the potty gradually with the goal that it will be a self-help skill, then our expectations, actions, and interactions are likely to be appropriate to individual children and effective for them as well. We are also able to put into perspective the inevitable ups and downs of group-care potty training, which helps us remain calm and maintain a relaxed atmosphere for children. This, of course, is important because toddlers do not need a tense environment—especially when they are in the midst of potty training. This book is based on our perspective, and we recommend it to you as you work through toilet training issues in your program.

How to Use This Book

Good Going! is organized into three main sections. The first (chapters 1, 2, and 3) addresses potty training from the child's perspective and offers appropriate program responses and practices. The second section (chapters 4, 5, and 6) focuses on creating a partnership with parents and dealing with hot-button issues—both those that caregivers may have with parents and those that parents may have with caregivers. The last section (chapter 7) focuses on creating policies and procedures about potty training. Program decision makers need the information, perspective, experiences, and suggestions presented in the first two sections of the book to create policies that will work well for their program, the staff, the parents, and the children.

In each section we have shared not only our suggestions, but also the thinking that led to those suggestions. Throughout the book you will find sample letters that you can use with parents to present potty training issues and information from the perspective in this book. We hope you will use them either as they are or as a guide to create your own for your program. You will also find that the potty training readiness indicators and information about clothing are presented in two versions. One version is for child care programs and providers. It contains more details and discussion. The other version is for parents. It is shorter and written in a more personal style. It also makes a great handout for parents.

Members of the Original Toilet Learning Task Force

Penny Feeney	Brittonfield Childcare Center
Amy Kelly	Brittonfield Childcare Center
Tracy Hodges	SonShine Child Care Center
Carrie Dumas	SonShine Child Care Center
Nancy Meunier	The Growing Place
Lisa Rouse	St. Vincent de Paul Day Care Center
Pam Patterson	St. Vincent de Paul Day Care Center
Linda Ricks	County North Children's Center
Leslei Anderson	County North Children's Center
Debbie Dufore	Salvation Army—Clinton Street Day Care Center
Heidi Joy	Salvation Army—Clinton Street Day Care Center
Linda Barbour	Ready-Set-Grow Day Care Center
Cheryl Livshin	Dewitt Child Development Center
Diane McMorris	Dewitt Child Development Center
Carol Baum	Dewitt Child Development Center
Tiffany Voss	Somewhere Special Child Care Center
Lynn Nash	Smart Day Care, Inc.
Fay Caples	Smart Day Care, Inc.
Sarah Roche	Nurturing World Child Care Center
Hannah Curle	Nurturing World Child Care Center
Pat Nye	Marcellus Presbyterian Child Care Center
Jean Wells	Marcellus Presbyterian Child Care Center
Camuna Azria	Little Learners Child Care Center
Betty LaVeck	Little Apples Child Care Center
Alissa McCall	Onondaga Community College Children's Center

A Special Note

Our original task force experienced the loss of one of its members, Heidi Joy, shortly after the last work session. We remember Heidi for her soft-spoken manner and her deep and genuine concern for children and parents. She made important contributions to the original booklet, and we were all saddened by her tragic death.

Readiness

The main question both parents and caregivers ask is, "When should children start potty training?" What most of us would like is a nice, easy, definite answer such as "at twenty-one months," or "three months after the child's first step." Some adults would like the answer to be, "When *I* decide it's time to start!"

This is one time, however, when we are not going to get the kind of answer we are looking for. Instead, experts from the pediatric and child development fields tell us that the answer is "when the child is ready." The American Academy of Pediatrics, for example, suggests that potty training should begin only when the child is developmentally ready or shows signs of readiness (American Academy of Pediatrics 1998). A pediatric textbook calls readiness the "key factor in successful toilet training" (Behrman, Kliegman, and Jenson 2000).

So how do we know when a child is ready? Experts have given us different age ranges when children are likely to be ready for potty training. Well-known pediatrician and researcher T. Berry Brazelton and others state that there is widespread agreement that a child should be ready to participate in toilet training at about eighteen months (Brazelton et al. 1999). Researchers from the University of Wisconsin concluded in a 1996 study that the age when a child is ready to be toilet trained is later—in the range of twenty-two to thirty months (Schum et al. 2002).

There is a big difference in the maturity of an eighteen-month-old child and a thirty-month-old child, but the researchers and experts in both cases emphasize the importance of looking at specific indications that an individual child is ready to begin the toilet training process. There is recognition that no two children will potty train on the same "correct timetable, and that there are predictable physical and behavioral clues that the child is ready" (Brazelton et al. 1999). These clues are the indicators that a child is ready to participate. These indicators don't give us an exact age or date to start potty training. Instead, they help us to identify a window of opportunity when starting is most likely to be successful.

This makes sense when we consider that for potty training to be a self-help skill, a child has to take an active role in it. And in order to take an active role, the child has to be ready and able.

So, what are the indicators that a child is ready? Here the experts are much more specific. They have identified physical, cognitive, and social-emotional indicators that a child is ready to begin potty training. The indicators and information related to them are listed here. A shorter, more personal version of the list for parents is in the appendix.

Readiness Indicators for Potty Training

Is the child at least eighteen months old?

Children develop the muscles and bladder capacity to begin the potty training process between the ages of eighteen and twenty-four months. It is at least useless, and possibly harmful, to expect any child to do something that she is physically unable to do.

Additional information: By eighteen months several physiological developments necessary for successful potty training are in place. Voluntary control over bowel and bladder reflex actions begins to emerge at nine months. By eighteen months sufficient neurological development allows some of the developmental energy required for walking and other gross-motor tasks to use in mastering toilet behavior (Brazelton et al. 1999).

For children to master potty training as a self-help skill, they must be able to consciously tighten their sphincter muscles so they can literally "hold it" until they can get to the potty. Children gradually master this between the ages of two and four, with 90 to 95 percent almost completely dry during the day and 80 to 85 percent almost completely dry at night by the age of five (Behrman 2000).

Are the child's diapers dry for at least two hours at a time?

Holding urine for at least two hours at a time indicates that the child's bladder is large enough and mature enough for potty training to be successful.

Additional information: Babies urinate as a reflex as often as fifteen to twenty times a day. Gradually the bladder enlarges, and the child develops conscious control over the bladder contractions and the external urinary sphincter muscles. A toddler whose bladder is ready for potty training will urinate large amounts at a time and then stay dry for several hours (Brazelton et al. 1999).

Does the child know—and let you know—when he is wet or has a bowel movement?

The child will not be able to successfully learn to use the toilet if he is not even aware of being wet or having had a bowel movement.

Does the child tell you or indicate that she is uncomfortable in wet or soiled diapers?

If the child feels quite comfortable with wet or soiled diapers, it will be hard to convince her to urinate and have bowel movements in the potty. A child who is ready to begin the potty training process will pull or tug at wet or soiled diapers or may indicate in another way that she is uncomfortable and wants to be changed.

Can the child sit upright for five minutes?

If the child is not able to sit anywhere for five minutes, he won't be able to sit on the potty long enough to urinate and have bowel movements—especially at first.

Can the child undress enough to sit on the potty?

The child needs to be able to do as much of the process independently as possible. She needs to be able to pull down her own pants so that toileting can become a self-help skill. It will be very hard for the child to get to the potty "in time" if she always has to wait for help with clothing from an adult.

Is the child able to get himself to the potty?

For toileting to be a self-help skill, the child needs to be able to take himself to the potty without help from an adult. A child who is walking should be stable enough on his feet to walk without assistance or holding onto furniture or walls.

Does the child follow simple directions?

The child will need to be able to follow directions and cooperate with you during this process. She needs to be able and willing (most of the time) to follow simple, one-step directions.

Does the child answer simple yes-and-no questions?

You will want the child to be able to communicate with you during this process, to be able to answer when adults ask if he is wet, ready to use the toilet, and so on.

Does the child imitate others—parents, caregivers, or other children?

The child who imitates other people—pretending to drink coffee like an adult, for example—will likely imitate others when it comes to potty training too.

Additional information: This is especially helpful in group care where there are likely to be other children in various stages of the potty training process.

Does the child trust and feel comfortable with the adults who care for her?

The child will have a difficult time learning this new skill if she doesn't trust the adults who are caring for her.

Does the child show pride, joy, or excitement when he learns new skills?

A child who shows pride, joy, or excitement in learning other new skills will approach potty training with the same feelings. A child who does not seem interested in accomplishing new tasks and mastering new skills may have trouble with potty training.

Do the adults—parents and caregivers—know what they will have to do to help the child learn to use the potty?

All the adults who are working with the child need to know what to expect during the potty training process. This will enable them to be supportive.

Additional information: Using the information in this book and the suggestions for sharing it with parents will ensure that parents and caregivers have common ground for carrying out the potty training process. Parents especially need to know how important consistency is and how difficult it is for children when adults have them go back and forth between being expected to use the potty and being put in diapers—whether they're cloth, disposable, or the pull-up type.

Are parents and caregivers willing and able to devote the time and attention to helping the child learn to use the potty?

Adults must make some changes in their routines, some sacrifices, and some time adjustments in order for the potty training process to be successful for the child.

Additional information: Adults who are not willing to make the adjustments necessary for potty training will very likely be setting up difficult situations for children. Maddening as it may be, potty training must be factored into the activities adults and families are planning. For example, children who have been working on potty training cannot all of a sudden be put back in diapers for a week because the family has planned a vacation and potty training will be inconvenient. Even an activity as simple as going to the store means that adults must either think about how their child can use a toilet while at the store or decide to have the child stay home rather than putting the child back in diapers for the trip to the store.

Special Circumstances That Can Affect a Child's Readiness

Sometimes all developmental indicators point to a child's readiness to begin the toilet training process. Before beginning, however, we should look at some factors that are not related to the child's development, but could greatly influence readiness. If toddlers are dealing with some of these issues, adults will need to think about whether to wait a bit until the child has had some time to adjust to the new situation before beginning potty training. You do not want to set up a child or yourselves for frustration because there are just too many changes for her to handle.

If any of the following are present, decide whether to proceed or to wait for a time. If you decide to begin the potty training process, proceed carefully. If you find a great deal of resistance from the child, consider waiting a few months and then trying again. Let the child adjust to one change before expecting him to be ready (or willing!) to take on a new one. Here are some of those factors:

- Have there been any recent changes in the household that seem difficult for the child?

    Has the child recently had a serious illness?
    Have the child's parents recently had a serious illness?
    Have the child's parents recently separated or divorced?
    Has there been a death in the family?
    Has the family moved recently?
    Is there a new baby in the family?

- Have there been any changes in the child's care?

    Did the child just begin at a child care program?
    Did the child recently change child care programs?
    Does the child have a new child care provider or caregiver?
    Did the child recently move to a new room in the child care program?

- Is the child in a very negative phase?

If the child is resisting adults in many other areas, she is likely to resist potty training as well.

When Parents' Needs Conflict with a Child's Readiness

Many of the members of our original task force had experiences with parents who wanted their children to be "potty trained" for reasons that had nothing to do with their child's readiness. Parents have asked that programs begin the process because

- "Diapers are so expensive!"
- "My mother-in-law says all her children were trained by the time they were twelve months old, and she wants to know why my child isn't trained yet."
- "I'm having a new baby in three months, and I don't want two in diapers at the same time."
- "All the other kids his age are potty trained."
- "My other children were all completely trained by the time they were as old as she is now."
- "I'm tired of changing diapers."
- "He goes in the potty at home, you know."

Here is the challenge for programs and caregivers: Programs really want to meet the needs of parents, but they also recognize the importance of the individual child's physical, intellectual, emotional, and social readiness to begin the toilet training process. If programs feel they need to set parents straight, they run the risk of alienating the parents and creating an atmosphere that will make it almost impossible to work together on anything. Fortunately, there are a number of ways programs and caregivers can work with parents who are ready for their children to start this process long before the children actually are ready.

First, programs and caregivers need to acknowledge what the parent is saying. It is important to realize that

- Diapers *are* expensive!
- A mother-in-law (or any relative or friend) *can* put a lot of pressure on parents to measure up.
- If you're expecting a new baby it *would* be nice to have the older child out of diapers.
- It *is* difficult when all the other children who are the same age as your child can do something your child can't.
- It *is* tempting to compare children and expect that if one was potty trained at a certain age, the other can be too.

Parents are not bad because they give these reasons for wanting their children to begin the potty training process; they are simply reflecting their needs. Caregivers who can understand where the parents are coming from and relate to them on that basis stand a much better chance of developing a partnership with them than caregivers who try to hit parents over the head with good child development theory.

Second, figure out how you could give parents some information about the potty training process in a way that would encourage them to wait and have the process go more quickly rather than insisting on starting before the child is ready and having the process take even longer. Of course, you will always have some parents who want (and fully expect) that they can start too early *and* have the process go very quickly. Point out that it would be wonderful if it worked like that, but it just doesn't. Most parents can also relate to the amount of stress this process will create—which is why they want to start potty training in the first place. Help parents realize that trying to start the process before the child is ready will result in lots of stress for the child, for you, and for them. Most people do not want to create more stress for themselves!

Third, figure out what you might be able to do. For example, if a parent of a fifteen-month-old wants her child to start the potty training process, consider that you could begin by helping the child become familiar with the potty. You could let the child observe other children using it or make available books about children using the potty. You could talk to the child about underwear even though the child is still in diapers. In this way, you are responding to the parent's need in a way that is appropriate to the child's developmental stage.

Fourth, consider having the parent talk to parents of other children in your program who have gone through the potty training process to share their experience.

Fifth, find resources in your community for parents to contact. Sometimes the opinion of someone not directly involved with the parent or the child carries more weight than that of the caregiver. Child care resource and referral agencies and pediatric practices are examples of such community resources.

Finally, it is still possible a parent may insist that starting the process means putting the child in underwear and strapping the child to the potty until she goes. This is where your program's policies will be helpful. As helpful as you want to be, you cannot (and would not want to) use such methods. The situation may come to the point where either the parent or the center recognizes that this program is not the right match for this family, which may happen even though the program presented its policies and procedures before the toilet learning process started.

When the Child Is Ready, but the Parents Aren't

As we mentioned in the introduction to this book, our original task force members struggled with parents who wanted their children potty trained before they were ready. In the years since that group met, we have encountered more situations when the child showed signs of readiness, but the parents did not want to start the process. We did not find that parents were saying, "I know that my child is ready for potty training, but I have decided that I don't want him to start." Rather, we heard from parents who were worried about either putting too much pressure on their children or parents who took a very hands-off approach and felt that eventually somehow their children would just kind of train themselves.

You need to be prepared to work with all parents—those whose expectations are in line with yours and those who have entirely different expectations. We have already addressed the parents who want their children trained early, but we also need to know what to do with the parents who aren't ready or willing to start the process.

When parents worry about putting too much pressure on their children, we need to understand and acknowledge that they have their child's interests at heart and are genuinely concerned about putting their child in a position that she can't handle. They may also be reacting to stories and anecdotes where adults *were* putting a lot of pressure on children during potty training. Parents of children who are by nature rather cautious may worry that their children will feel pressured by potty training even if the method used is appropriate. Their feelings and their worries, then, are entirely understandable.

There are several ways you can help parents who are concerned about pressure surrounding potty training. First, make sure you are using solid readiness indicators and that both the parents and you are using them. This will give everyone a very good sense of the child's ability to begin and handle potty training. Second, if the method you will be using at the program—and the corresponding method being used at home—is based on the method presented in this book, then you expect that children will gradually master potty training as a self-help skill. The "gradual" part of this perspective means that the child will be able to learn at his own pace. Finally, if you are using this perspective, you will not use any potty training methods that are harsh or punitive. When parents know that you have a well-developed, thoughtful, appropriate approach to potty training, they may feel more confident that their child will not be harmed by undue pressure.

Parents who just want to let children train themselves may actually believe that this will happen all by itself or they truly may not want to be bothered with the whole process. You need to help them see that potty training is both a matter of developmental readiness and learning skills. To learn the various potty training skills, children need support from adults. This support includes advice and instruction, encouragement and expectations, and opportunities to practice. Especially in group care, toddlers will see what other children are doing with potty training. Since they are such great imitators, they will want to try it themselves. And if all other indications are that they are ready to begin, why should we stop them? If parents see that the quickest way for their children to master potty training is to give them all the support they need once they are ready, parents may be more willing to play their important role.

Programs that expect parents and caregivers to work together when children are learning to use the toilet will also have a structure in place so those partnerships can happen. These programs are then likely to be successful with all parents including those who may want to start too early and those who may not want to start at all.

2

Potty Training Routines in Group Care Programs

When children are in a group setting, it can be difficult to come up with a potty training method or routine that works well for both the staff and individual children. You really can't have restrictions on when children can use the potty, and so rigid, required "potty times" aren't a good idea. At the same time, it will not help children master potty training as a self-help skill to have staff following children around, constantly asking them if they have to go. The caregivers in our original task force recommend the following routine that respects the needs of individual children and is also practical for staff to carry out.

Phase One: Getting Started

- Chart the diapering/toileting of individual children. Keep a record of when the child is wet, dry, or has a bowel movement. When you start to see a pattern in which a child is consistently dry for at least two hours at a time, go to phase two.
- Use the information from the chart to establish a schedule for that child's diaper changing. For example, if you notice that a child is always dry between 9:00 and 10:30 A.M., but is usually wet by 11:00, you may decide to change the child at 10:30. As part of the changing process, encourage the child to sit on the potty. Diaper changing, then, includes taking off the diaper (which is still dry), sitting on the potty with the possibility that the child will urinate, and then putting on a clean diaper.

Phase Two: The Child Is Ready to Start

After parents and caregivers have considered the readiness questions and agree that the child is ready, consider the following steps:

- Talk to parents about toileting routines in the center. Tell parents when the child typically uses the toilet at the center and find out when she is using it at home.

- Agree on a potty training procedure that can be carried out both at home and in the program. Remember that consistency is very important for success.
- Have the child begin to wear training pants. Have parents bring in lots of extra clothing. The child should have extra training pants, pants, socks and shoes, and shirts. (Additional information about clothing can be found on page 32.)
- Unless the child is already taking himself to the potty, suggest to the child going potty at regular intervals. You already have children at different stages of the process in your group. This means there will probably already be a group that is going to the potty at these regular intervals. This should help children just beginning the process since toddlers are great imitators. Those new to the process will have a wonderful opportunity to see that others are using the potty on a regular basis.

Announcing potty time sets up the expectation that the child will go, and establishes potty time as a regular part of the day. This will work better than asking toddlers if they have to go potty for several reasons. Asking, "Do you have to (or want to) go potty?" sets up the opportunity for the child to say no even when he may need to go to the potty. Most of us then say, "Are you *sure* you don't have to go potty?" The toddler may give us a response that roughly translates to "Yes, I'm sure." Then we say, "No, you're not," which is too confusing and too likely to produce resistance from toddlers. Here are some good ways to announce potty time:

> It's potty time. I'll sing a song while we get ready to go to the potty.

> It's almost time for lunch. Let's go potty and wash our hands before we eat.

> We had such a good time on our walk. As soon as we get back to our room, we'll have potty time.

> It's potty time. You can bring your toys over here to the potty room door. We'll put them on this chair so they can wait right here while you use the potty.

Several programs suggest using a timer to indicate potty time. Some caregivers initially set it to ring every hour; others set the timer a few minutes before they would like it to ring. One caregiver advised having children help set the timer and talking about how it will remind everyone to use the potty. Using a timer is something that can also be done at home.

- If a child wets or has a bowel movement in her pants, clean her up immediately while reassuring the child that it is all right. It is important that you and the parents really do accept these accidents as inevitable. It is annoying to have to clean up the child and wash all the clothes, but it is part of the learning process for the child. Fighting the inevitable accidents or punishing the child for them will certainly slow the process.

  While you don't want to browbeat children for having accidents, you also want to send the message that they need to use the potty and that you believe they are capable of doing it. You might say, "Oh, I see your pants are wet. Let's change you. The next time you have to pee, you can go on the potty."

  Notice that this approach does not start with asking the child, "Are you wet?" Some children may feel ashamed that they wet their pants and may answer no, so they won't have to admit it. Guilt and shame are not effective ways of helping young children learn new skills, so adults simply cannot shame a child to stop having accidents.

- Encourage children to take themselves to the potty whenever they have to go. Tell them, "We'll always have some potty time. You can go then, and you can go any other time when you have to go."

Helpful Hints

You can help individual toddlers with the toileting process by making your own stories about how they use the potty. These stories should be short, personal descriptions of the toileting process. They can then be used at potty time or any time children may want to hear them. They are a great way to share information with parents too. You can make a copy of the story and send it home for parents. Here is an example of such a story:

> Mia started using the potty when she pees and has a bowel movement. When Jenny says, "It's potty time!" Mia goes to the potty. She can pull down her own pants and then she sits on the potty. She likes to read a book while she sits on the potty. Sometimes she pees in the potty and sometimes she has a bowel movement. When she is done, she wipes herself. Then she flushes; she likes to watch the water go round and round in the potty. Then Mia washes her hands. She uses the pumper soap and a lot of water. Mia likes to say, "Ta Da!" when she's done. And that's the end of potty time.

Keep in mind that these stories will change as children's abilities change. They can also be a way to communicate expectations and next steps to children. Here is an example:

Mia goes to the potty when Jenny says, "It's potty time!" Pretty soon Mia will decide when to go to the potty all by herself. She knows how to do it. She can walk to the potty, pull down her pants, pee or have a BM, and then flush and wash her hands. Then she will come out and say, "I did it." And Jenny will smile because Mia did it all by herself.

If little boys are learning to urinate standing up, put a square of toilet paper in the potty for them to aim at. Many programs report that they have boys start by sitting backwards on the potty to urinate before they try to do it standing up.

Children may realize that you watch them while they go to the potty. They may see their parents in the bathroom at home. It is not surprising, then, if they ask you, "Can I watch you go potty?"

Here's a great answer: "No. I like to go potty by myself. I know how to do everything in the bathroom, so I just go all by myself."

3

Bathroom Design and Equipment

Design: Access, Supervision, and Privacy

Many of the original task force members worked in centers located in buildings that had originally served other functions. Their rooms—even the toddler rooms—were unlikely to have bathrooms in them. Since then several new centers have been built in our community with nice, practical toileting areas right in the classrooms, but others are still in older buildings without them. In family child care settings, providers typically use the bathroom in their home as the children's toileting area. Whatever the situation, you need to think about how the toileting area is designed, what kind of equipment is in it, how to supervise children when they are toileting, and how to deal with varying privacy needs.

The toileting area needs to be accessible to children. When children realize they need to use the toilet and then take themselves to the bathroom, they should not have to ask for help opening a door or lowering a toilet seat. The toileting area needs to provide for both supervision and privacy for children who want or need it. While these may appear at first to be mutually exclusive, both can be accommodated in several ways. Some child care centers have bathrooms with half doors so children have privacy while adults can see in from above. Other centers use low partitions to separate the toilet or potty from the rest of the bathroom. The bathrooms have a changing area, a sink, and a toileting area. A child using the toilet has a sense of privacy while the adult can supervise. The other areas of the bathroom can be used at the same time a child is on the toilet or potty.

Programs without a bathroom in their room face a special problem. Children cannot leave the room to go to the bathroom by themselves since they must always have adult supervision. However, when children are learning to use the toilet, they need access to the bathroom when *they* feel the need to go. Caregivers may take groups to the bathroom at certain times, but they also need to develop a plan that allows them to meet the needs of children who indicate they have to use the bathroom at other times. When we understand potty training to be a developmental process and help children master it as a self-help skill, we strive to help them understand their bodies' signals and experience success in interpreting and acting on those signals. We can tailor our actions to the needs of individual children at different stages in the self-help process. Children near the end may indeed be able to "hold it" for a few minutes before a regularly scheduled trip to the bathroom. Children closer to the beginning of the process are probably not able to hold it. They've gotta go when they've gotta go!

This is an example of one time when what is good and necessary for children is certainly not very convenient for adults. But the emphasis should be on children's success at learning to use the toilet, rather than on the number of trips to the bathroom we make with them each day. This is also a time when program administrators need to be aware of the staffing needs in the toddler room. When there are several toddlers beginning the potty training process, a toddler room may need an additional caregiver so that children who need to go to the bathroom can be taken, while other children in the program are adequately supervised.

Equipment: Toilets, Potty Chairs, and Potty Seats

While "cute" is not usually the first word we think of in relation to potty training, the new child-size toilets that are about six inches off the ground are just that. They are ideal because they look exactly like the toilets children see at home, yet are just the right size for children and much more sanitary than potty chairs. When child care centers are being built or renovated, these tiny toilets are almost always included. Many toddlers, however, are in programs that don't have these toilets.

When toddlers are in family child care settings, it is likely that they will be using the small potty chairs specifically designed for children. Like all potty training equipment, potty chairs should be safe and easily accessible to children. The potty should be child-size, have a wide enough base, and be heavy enough so that it will not tip over or stick to children when they stand up after using it. It is especially important that children feel secure and safe when using the potty. Therefore, they should be able to put both feet securely on the floor or on a stable step when sitting on the potty. Being able to have both feet securely on the floor also helps children push when they are trying to have bowel movements. For this reason, the original task force recommended that child care providers not use special potty seats that attach to or sit on top of regular toilet seats. If such a seat is the only option, children will need to have a sturdy step to reach it and to use for balance, security, and pushing.

Our task force members were also cautious about potty chairs or seats with deflectors or shields that stick up from the seat. While we understood that the deflectors were designed to keep little boys from urinating out of the potty while sitting down, several members of the task force had children who had injured themselves on the deflectors while trying to sit down or get up from these seats. They found a potty chair with a front that was higher than the back and felt that it worked just as well and was easier and safer for the children to use.

It is also very important that potties be easy to clean. In group care, potties really must be emptied and cleaned by adults because children are not able to do this task well enough to meet hygiene standards. Children who empty their own potties at home or help their parents may be quite insistent that they also do it in their child care program. Understandable. Caregivers may need to have a friendly, but matter-of-fact statement ready for this situation as well as something the child *can* do. Try, "At home *you* empty the potty, and here *I* empty the potty." Perhaps the child could do one of the following:

- Tell the caregiver to empty the potty or answer, "Yes!" when the caregiver asks, "Should I empty the potty now?"
- Clap after the caregiver empties the potty.
- Stand ready to flush.

Potty chairs should be placed in an area that is inviting to children. There should be enough light so children won't be worried about the dark. Caregivers can make the area more inviting to children by putting pictures or designs on the walls at the children's eye level. The area must also be one where the caregiver can supervise children easily.

It is important to recognize that some children want and need privacy when using the toilet. Adults might be tempted to regard privacy for children as unimportant. We sometimes hear adults say, "What's the big deal? It's not like I'm going to see something I haven't seen before!" The desire or need for privacy belongs to the individual. Adults have different needs concerning privacy and different levels of tolerance for lack of privacy. Children are the same. We need to be as aware and respectful of it in children as we are in adults.

Hygiene during Potty Training

Following good hygiene procedures when dealing with the toilet is always important. However, in group care situations it is absolutely critical that you follow such procedures scrupulously and consistently. When children are learning to use the toilet, the following procedures must be in place.

- **Children must wash their hands each time they use the toilet or potty.**
  It will be important for you to help children understand that they need to wash their hands even if they did not actually urinate or have a bowel movement while they were sitting on the

potty. It is also important that hand washing gradually become a self-help skill for children involved in the potty training process. Children will need a great deal of guidance and instruction from you when it comes to hand washing. You'll probably have to spend some time with toddlers washing their hands, talking about hand washing, and gradually helping them do it all by themselves. Children must be able to reach and use all the supplies and equipment to wash their hands in order for hand washing to become a self-help skill.

Hand washing is an easy way for parents to help maintain consistency between home and child care during the potty training process. Share your hand-washing procedures with parents and encourage them to use the same practices at home.

Besides making sure children wash their hands, you must make sure you wash your own hands each time you have contact with the toilet, potty, or clothing that has been wet or soiled. Ideally you should have single-use latex gloves, but if they are not available, the type of gloves used for food service are better than no gloves at all.

● **The toilet must be flushed or the potty emptied. Potties must be disinfected after each use.**

Some children like to flush the toilet and some are wary of flushing. Make sure you respect the concerns of those children who may be wary. After all, if you really think about it, there's really quite a lot to worry about. First, it's noisy. Then, there is a whole lot of water swirling around very suddenly in a bowl that is bigger around than you are, and, finally, whatever is in that toilet is sucked away and is gone forever to who knows where. From this perspective, it's a little easier to consider that children who are wary of flushing are being quite thoughtful and really quite reasonable. This understanding will help you be more effective with them. You should *allow* children who like flushing to flush, but don't demand it from children who are afraid of flushing. You can help children who are wary of flushing by letting them observe flushing from a distance they feel is safe for them. Some children may want to practice flushing something other than their own bodily secretions. Let them flush pieces of toilet paper if they would like to try flushing.

● **The toilet seat should be disinfected by being wiped off, sprayed with a bleach and water solution, and allowed to air dry.**

(To make the bleach and water solution, mix one tablespoon of bleach in a quart of water in a spray bottle. This should be made up daily.) A potty should be emptied, rinsed, and disinfected after each child uses it. This task really must be done by adults. Children are simply not able to clean the toilet or potty well enough to meet group care hygiene considerations, nor do we want them handling the bleach and water solution.

The walls and floor in the toileting area should be kept clean and disinfected with the bleach and water solution. This can become quite a task when little boys are learning to urinate while standing up. You can help them out by putting up an interesting picture at eye level above the potty, so they will be more likely to be faced in the right direction. You can also let them aim at little squares of toilet paper in the potty. Don't distract them by calling their name while they are urinating standing up. They will turn their heads to look at you and all other body parts will follow.

● **Clothing in which a child has had a bowel movement should be put into a plastic bag without being rinsed.**

Rinsing the clothing increases the likelihood of spreading infection.

● **Proper wiping needs to be taught.**

We suggest that you take turns with toddlers so that they are wiped well enough while they gradually learn to wipe themselves. Start by taking the first two turns yourself, then trading turns with the toddler. Teach children how to tell when they are done wiping. As long as there is brown on the toilet paper, there is still more to wipe. When the toilet paper no longer has any brown on it, wiping is complete. Girls should be taught to wipe from front to back.

You can help children remember good hygiene practices and also help them learn to follow directions by using a "to do" list. Here is a sample. When you say it every time children use the potty, they will learn it. Put up your fingers for each of the three steps as an added visual clue. As they get older you can say part of it and see if children can fill in the rest.

After I go potty, I wipe myself,
I flush the potty, and I wash my hands.
1–2–3 ! Wipe, flush, wash!

Developing Partnerships with Parents

Perhaps more than almost any other issue, potty training has the potential to produce disagreements and even clashes between parents and caregivers. This is hardly surprising when we realize that parents form their understandings and expectations about potty training based on their cultures, their own upbringing, advice from their families, and perhaps from what they have read. They bring these to caregivers and programs that have their own understandings and expectations based on the child care culture. If the understandings and expectations of the parents and the child care program match or are pretty close, potty training will probably go quite smoothly. If they are very different, the parents and the caregivers might not have an easy time forming a partnership, and this in turn could make the process more difficult for the child.

We believe that many problems for children and conflicts between parents and caregivers over potty training can be avoided. We also believe that programs must take the initiative in working with parents to develop partnerships for their children's toilet learning. Child care programs and toddler caregivers are always in a potty training mode and are likely to know what they need to discuss with parents. Work on such partnerships needs to start before the potty training process and begin with the understandings and expectations of both the parents and the program.

It would be impossible for a child care program or caregivers to know the practices of every culture of every family they will ever serve. It would also be wrong to assume that all parents from a particular culture have the same understandings and expectations about potty training. The best way for programs and caregivers to learn what parents think and believe about potty training is to ask and listen to their responses.

We must also recognize that child care has a culture of its own. One of the main aspects of this culture is having a group of same-age children with one adult caring for them, which means that caregivers are not able to give children as much one-on-one attention as their parents can. Children are expected to do more for themselves. Children in group care can observe and imitate other children and may be able and willing to do things that amaze their parents. Another part of the child care culture relevant to potty training is that caregivers can individualize only within the structure of the program. In potty training, for example, caregivers cannot have completely different methods for each child. They can, however, use the program's selected potty training method on an individualized basis with children at each child's level. Finally, the most important part of the child care culture is what it feels like to be in the program. If a program has a culture of acceptance, children and parents will feel valued. Parents will know it is safe to bring up questions and to make suggestions. Caregivers will know how to respond to those questions and suggestions even if the answer is not what the parents want to hear. The following suggestions for activities and timetable will help programs develop partnerships with parents.

Before meeting with parents, compile all information, checklists, hand-outs, and policies you want to use in developing the partnership. A great deal of information in this book can be used for this purpose.

Parents should know how the program approaches potty training. This information should be available to parents at a number of points. It might be included in the parent handbook. There might be a short, introductory statement about potty training in the letter or information parents get when children move into the toddler room or when children reach certain developmental milestones ("Now that your child has started walking . . ."). This statement would come well before the child actually begins potty training, but it sets the stage for parents.

Here is a sample of such a statement:

> One of the skills children begin working on in this room is potty train-ing. It can be quite a challenge to potty train several toddlers at the same time, but we've done our homework, and we've got some prac-tices and approaches that work pretty well. We've also got some good information for you and some questions so you can give us informa-tion too. We'll have to work together on a finding a good time for your child to start potty training. We'll be talking to you about this soon. If you can't wait to hear about it, come and talk to us.

You also should plan to give parents a letter about readiness that includes the readiness questions. You might give the letter to parents when their children turn a certain age or a certain amount of time after children have entered the room where potty training usually occurs. The sample "readiness letter" is on page 23. The readiness questions are in the appendix.

Dear Parents,

You are looking forward to having your child learn to use the toilet. You probably feel that you just can't wait for your child to be out of diapers and using the toilet all by herself. At our program we look at potty training as a skill your child will learn gradually. At first children in our program need lots of help and gradually they are able to do more and more themselves. This is our goal: your child will be able to handle toileting all by herself. This means that your child will be actively participating in potty training; we won't be doing everything for her. This is usually a pretty good fit for toddlers because they want to be independent and are trying to do more and more for themselves. We hear them loud and clear, "Me do it!" We want your child to be successful at potty training, so we pay attention to making sure she is ready—that all systems are go—and that all of us are ready to support her.

So, when do we start and what do we do? We use a list of questions that will help us know when your child has the physical development, the understanding, and the motivation to start learning to use the toilet. We would like to look at the list with you and then discuss your ideas about potty training and share our ideas and practices with you.

We want to work together on this because your child will be learning to use the toilet both at home and at our program. Children can't succeed if the expectations and practices change from place to place and adult to adult.

Please let us know when you are ready to consider potty training for your child. If we notice signs that she may be ready, we may contact you first. Either way, we'll work together so she can master this important skill.

Sincerely,

We recommend that the potty training process begin with a discussion between parents and their child's caregivers. At any time after the child is fifteen months old, either you or the parents can initiate this discussion. Although physical indicators for potty training are present as early as eighteen months, parents and caregivers can certainly begin talking about the process before that. What most people consider actual potty training, including having children in training pants and sitting on the potty, generally can't start before eighteen months, but many parents are ready to ask about it earlier. This discussion really needs to be like a miniconference, not just a quick word while parents are picking up their children. It doesn't have to take long, but should be an opportunity for parents and caregivers to compare notes on the child and to start with a clear understanding of what to expect from each other.

At this conference the parents and caregivers should share information about the child, the potty training process, the parents' ideas and concerns about potty training, and the program's potty training practices. Make sure parents have all the compiled information on potty training. The purpose of this initial conference is to make sure parents and caregivers have the same understanding about the potty training process. Review the readiness indicators together and both keep a copy to use as you observe the child.

When the child is ready to begin, have a second conference to discuss how to talk with the child, begin the process, provide consistency between home and the program, handle communication, and discuss any other issues you have.

Here's a suggested format for the second conference:

- **Review the readiness indicators together.**
  If there is a discrepancy between what parents observe at home and what you observe at the program, share observations and anecdotes. The child really needs to exhibit readiness at both locations for the process to be successful. If the indicators are not present, see if some of them can be encouraged and spend the rest of the time talking about how this might happen. (This is in the section on readiness.) If the readiness indicators are present, continue and cover the following topics.

- **Talk about the importance of consistency between the program and home.**
  Everyone needs to agree to use the same procedures in this process. It is very important that a child not wear training pants at one place and diapers at the other or that a child is expected to use the potty at one place and it's optional at the other. Once the process starts, everyone working with the child needs to cooperate. Recognize that, quite likely, adults will

become weary (and wet!) during this process, but also recognize that consistency is essential for the child to be successful. Encourage parents to think and talk about how they'll handle situations such as trips to the store while their child is learning to use the potty. Parents may think it is simple, logical, and harmless to just put a diaper (even the pull-up disposable diapers) on their child for that short time, but it often backfires. Children aren't sure what we really want them to do. Are they supposed to use the potty or not? If they are, then why are we putting them back in diapers? Are diapers the only safe place to urinate and have bowel movements? We have worked with some children who are over four years old and absolutely never wet or soil their underwear, but they will also not sit on the potty. When they need to urinate or have a bowel movement, they insist on having disposable pull-up diapers. These are very smart children, and they learn very well. They just learned the wrong thing. That's not what their parents meant to teach them, but they did. It is helpful here to use the perspective that is in this book because it is always pointing us in the direction of helping toileting become a self-help skill for children. If we go back and forth between "now you are supposed to use the potty" and "now you can just wear a diaper," children can't tell what direction we want them to go.

- **Talk about the importance of ongoing communication between the program and home.**
  Agree on a communication method to share questions and concerns, victories and setbacks. It can be difficult for parents or caregivers to talk at pick-up time, and adults should not be discussing a child's problems in front of the children. Perhaps this communication could take place with phone calls or with notes if face-to-face conversations are not possible.

- **Discuss hygiene practices.**
  Explain to parents about not rinsing bowel movements out of clothes at the program. Talk with parents about helping and teaching children to wipe themselves and about the importance of hand washing. Share your hand-washing routines so parents can use them at home too. Additional information about hygiene practices can be found on page 17.

- **Talk about clothing.**
  Talk with parents about appropriate clothing (information can be found in chapter 6) and requirements for extra clothing. Parents and caregivers should come to an understanding

about how and when diapers, training pants, and underwear will be used.

- **Consider the equipment.**

  Parents and caregivers should know what kind of toilet, toilet seat, or potty the child will be using at home and at the program. This can really become a difficult issue for some children who don't like one kind of potty at home and another kind at the program, so parents and caregivers may have to think of ways to talk to the child about it. For a little boy, parents and caregivers should agree on whether he will learn to urinate standing up or sitting down. We have found that while parents may have a preference about this, many boys imitated other boys at the program.

- **Use the same language.**

  Caregivers and parents should choose toileting words that the child can say easily. While some adults may wish to use *urinate* and *defecate,* those words may be too difficult for young children to pronounce. The more children can talk and ask about what is happening, the more potty training can become a self-help skill. So we need to make sure that the words we use are words they will be able to use themselves. Members of our task force found that *pee, wet, poop, BM,* and *go potty* all worked well with young children. These toileting words should be used both at home and in the program. Many families have certain phrases—almost like pet terms—for bowel movements. Just among our own group, we remembered that our own families used a variety of terms including *boom, big-jobbie,* and *making a cigar.* These may work just fine when children are being potty trained only at home, but not when they are learning to use the toilet both at home and at a child care program. A young child who announces to a caregiver, "I hafta boom!" is absolutely certain that he has communicated clearly and correctly. This puts both the caregiver and the child in a difficult position, and may result in an accident that could have been easily prevented.

- **Talk about dealing with accidents.**

  Parents and caregivers should talk about accidents as an inevitable part of the potty training process. Parents and caregivers should agree on acceptable, effective ways to handle these accidents. (Information on this topic can be found on page 40.)

● **Discuss how to deal with pressure or signs of distress in the child and the possibility of stopping the process for a while.**

Excessive pressure must not be placed on a child to use the toilet by either parents or caregivers. All adults must watch for signs of distress in the child, such as anxiety, withdrawing, refusing to use the toilet, or holding back bowel movements. In such cases, the adults should agree to stop the process and wait until the child is more at ease. This decision must be made thoughtfully because it is confusing for young children to stop and start potty training several times.

Clothing

Our original task force had identified clothing as one of the issues we wanted to work on. As soon as we began our discussion we realized that this was one of the hottest hot buttons. Members of the task force said that problems related to clothing were among the most frustrating issues they had with parents. They mentioned two specific problems.

- Parents often dress toddlers in clothes that even Houdini couldn't get out of in time to use the potty.
- Some parents do not send an adequate supply of extra clothes so children can be changed after accidents.

On the surface, these issues seem so straightforward and so simple to solve. For the first one, tell parents what their children should and should not wear. For the second one, lay down the law. Make a list of required clothes, and if parents don't send them in . . . this is where it gets sticky. What would we do? Put the parents in time-out? Ground them? Fine them? Kick them out of our program?

We quickly realized that these issues are not as straightforward as they seem and are nowhere near as simple to solve as we thought. We began by tackling the first problem. We started by considering why so many parents dressed their children in clothing that was very difficult to remove. We did some serious thinking, and we discovered several things:

- Most parents aren't even aware clothing is a problem.
- Many parents believe that adults in the child care program undress the children each time they use the potty.
- The cutest clothes on the market for toddlers are usually also at the top of our "worst for potty training" list.
- Many parents take great pride in having fashionable clothing for their children—even toddlers.
- Parents don't want to be told how they can and cannot dress their children.
- Most programs don't give parents any guidance at all when it comes to the clothes that are easy during potty training and that ones that are difficult for children.

We had a situation that was bothering us because we expected parents to know that choosing appropriate clothing would be important for potty training. But parents, it turned out, really hadn't thought about it. This may be annoying to us, but it is hardly surprising. First, most parents simply do not do the amount of potty training that we do. They are only caring for their own children—and it is rare to find parents who have more than two or three children these days. We, on the other hand, are caring for many children. Year after year we continue to have toddlers, and we have them in groups. We know how important appropriate clothing is for potty training because we work with it every day. All this information is new to parents, and they may well have bought their children's clothing without giving potty training a thought. Imagine that! They are out there buying clothes just on the basis of how cute their children will look!

We found that the first time most of us talked with parents about clothing was *after* we had struggled with their children's clothes. This, of course, was after they had bought their toddler's wardrobe. We had to admit that some of us used a "you should know better, after all this is just common sense" tone when we approached parents about the clothing issue. We also found that parents did not respond very well to these conversations. They felt that we were trying to tell them how they could or could not dress their children.

We realized that we had not been sharing what we knew about clothing with parents *before* it became an issue. We decided that the best approach would be to help parents understand the need for their children to be able to manage their own clothing and to help them see how certain clothing styles helped or hindered their children. We drafted a letter for parents that was all about clothing and could be given to them before they went out and bought a wardrobe of bib overalls. We also compiled two lists of clothing—good clothes and bad clothes. It didn't take long for us to realize that these lists might not go over very well with parents, so we tried to think of how to present the information in a way that parents would welcome. We decided to change the names of the lists. They became "clothing that will help children master potty training" and "clothing that will make potty training difficult for children." Our letter for parents and our clothing lists follow.

Dear Parents,

Now that your child will be learning to use the potty, you want to make sure that he has clothes that make this process as easy as possible for him. Especially at the beginning, the time between when your child realizes that he needs to urinate and when he actually does it will be very, very short. He won't have to time to struggle with his clothes. It will be discouraging for him to realize he needs to use the toilet and then wet the floor because he couldn't get his clothes off fast enough. As you know, we look at potty training as an important self-help skill for toddlers. Being able to get his own clothes off and on so he can go when he needs to go, all by himself, is very important. Potty training can't become a self-help skill if he can only accomplish it when an adult is available to undo buttons, snaps, and buckles.

We have included a list of clothes to help your child during potty training. We've also included a list of clothes that could make things very difficult. These lists are from parents and teachers with years of potty training experience, who want to share what they've learned with you. Unfortunately, some of these clothes—often the cutest toddler clothes on the market—are the very ones that give toddlers the most trouble when they're learning to use the potty. It is so important for your child to have clothing that he can manage by himself that it is worth using such outfits only on special occasions or putting them away until he can undo all the snaps, buttons, or buckles.

As your child begins learning to use the toilet, we recommend thickly padded training pants. As he experiences success, you can switch to thinner underwear with plastic pants and then to thinner underwear by itself.

We will change your child whenever he is wet or has a bowel movement. We will never allow him to remain in wet or soiled clothes. This means we will be doing a lot of changing at the beginning of the process, which means he will need a lot of extra clothes. We will need at least five pairs of training pants, three pairs of socks, three pairs of pants, and extra shoes available at all times.

If your child runs out of clothes, we will use extra clothing we keep here for this purpose. It is important that you wash and return the clothing. We won't use your child's clothing for other children, and we won't use other children's clothing for your child. It may be tempting to think that if your child only has one set of clean clothes, he will realize that he can't have any accidents and so will be sure not to wet himself. This may seem logical, but only to adults. Young children don't think in those terms. They learn by trial and error (and there will be lots of errors) and by experiencing success.

When your child wets or has a bowel movement in his clothing, we will put it in a plastic bag without rinsing it out. This often surprises parents, and we know that it would be much more convenient for you to get clothing that has been rinsed out. However, we are following recommended standards for infection control which specify that child care centers not rinse out clothing after children urinate, have bowel movements, or vomit in them.

We know this may seem like a lot of extra work, but it is only for a short time, and the rewards for you and your child will be well worth the extra work.

Yours,

Clothing that will help children master potty training

- **Elastic-waist, loose-fitting pants**
  We recommend these pants over those with buttons or snaps because they are easy for children to pull up and down themselves.

- **Waist-length undershirts**
  Longer undershirts interfere with the toileting process.

- **Thickly padded cotton training pants**
  Use thickly padded training pants when potty training starts. They absorb better when children have accidents, and children can pull them up and down themselves.

- **Regular underwear**
  As children experience success, allow them to wear underwear. Children can easily pull the underwear up and down themselves; they also give immediate feedback when children have accidents. Underwear must not be a reward for learning to use the potty. It should be considered one of the tools.

- **Lots of extra clothes including training pants, extra pants, socks, and shoes**
  We want to be able to clean children up as quickly as possible and with as little fuss as possible. Children must never be forced to stay in clothes that are wet or have a bowel movement in them.

Clothing that makes potty training difficult for children

- **Bib overalls or pants with belts, buckles, snaps, or buttons**
  Many toddlers may not have the fine-motor skills or the finger strength to unfasten these on their own.

- **Tight-fitting pants**
  Many toddlers may not have the strength, patience, or coordination to pull them down. If they get wet, many adults may not have the strength, patience, or coordination to pull them off.

- **One-piece outfits and jumpsuits**
  One-piece outfits require a lot of time to get off. Some of the jump suits that snap in the crotch, but not all the way down the legs, are especially difficult to get out of. These outfits also leave you practically naked just to pee!

- **Onesie-type undershirts or bodysuits**
  Many toddlers cannot unsnap these shirts. In addition, the long backs frequently fall in the toilet and get wet. Children may feel that they have failed because their clothes got wet even though they got all the urine in the potty.

- **Dresses, skirts, and tights**
  Toileting can be difficult when little girls try to use one hand to hold the dress or skirt up and have only one hand available to pull down panties. Tights are usually difficult to pull down and seem especially difficult to pull back up. Skirts can work if they can be pulled up and down easily like slacks.

- **Pull-up type disposable diapers**
  Disposable, pull-up type diapers are marketed as a type of underwear that is especially good for potty training. They may be designed to look like underwear but they function like a diaper, making it very hard for toddlers to feel when they are wet. Toddlers then have a difficult time making the connection between the feeling of a full bladder and the need to use the potty.

A Special Discussion about Disposable Diapers That Pull Up

The members of our original task force were so emphatic and united in their dislike of the disposable diapers that pull up that we decided to have a special section about them. We have found that nearly all caregivers share this opinion.

Some people approach the issue of disposable diapers from an environmental point of view and urge parents not to use them. We would like to approach the issue of disposable diapers during potty training from the perspective presented earlier in this book.

We see potty training as a process that helps children master toileting as a self-help skill. When children are in the process of potty training, one of the skills they must master is knowing when they have to urinate or have a bowel movement. If they don't figure this out, then adults must always take them to the potty, and toileting won't be a self-help skill.

How will children know this? Let's take a look at how adults know. We feel that our bladders or bowels are full and then we know that we are going to have to go to the toilet to empty them. We use our body's built-in indicator to figure this out, and this indicator works pretty well. Toddlers are learning about this built-in indicator and how to use it to know when they should go to the potty.

There are a couple of steps here. First, they have to realize when they have urinated or have had a bowel movement. Adults often point this out to toddlers. The adults might feel the sudden warmth of urine while they are holding children or see children straining to move their bowels or smell that a child has just had a bowel movement. When adults say, "Oh, I think you're peeing right now!" or "You just had a big BM," they are giving very useful feedback to toddlers because it helps the toddlers put words with actions. This can help them during the potty training process and they will become familiar with the language of toileting. This will help them understand and talk about what is going on while they are learning to use the toilet.

Eventually, however, what we want is for children to be able to feel for themselves that they *are* wet or have had a bowel movement rather than relying on outside feedback. Once they can tell that they are wet or soiled by the feeling, they will begin to figure out what it feels like right *before* they wet or have a bowel movement. They will have figured out the body's built-in indicator. And this is a huge step in having toileting become a self-help skill. Most of us who potty train toddlers have experienced that "Aha!" moment when a child realizes for the first time that he feels like he has to urinate before he actually does. There is often an expression of surprise as the child jumps up and announces, "Potty, potty, potty!"

Cloth diapers or heavy training pants are absorbent, but they also allow children to feel that they are wet. Disposable diapers are now designed for such comfort that children may not be able to feel wetness. And if they can't feel the wetness, they won't be able to tell that they have wet and, in turn, will have a difficult time with the body's internal indicator.

There are some disposable diapers that turn color when they are wet, and some people feel that this is a wonderful way for children to figure out that they have wet. But if we think about this a little more, we might get a different picture. None of us as adults walk around asking ourselves, "I wonder if I already peed? Let me look at the band of my underwear and see if it has turned color."

The disposable diapers that pull up are marketed as underwear that will help children during potty training. But they are really diapers. (Think about it. If they're just like underwear, why not just use underwear? We use them for the very same reason that we use other diapers.) Using these diapers that pull up during potty training sends a message to children, and that message is, "We say we want you to learn to use the toilet, but we're going to put diapers on you anyway."

Other Clothing Issues

You may find that some parents cannot or will not send enough extra clothes for their children during the potty training process. Some parents might not be able to afford the additional clothes. Others may believe that if their daughter only has one set of clean clothes, she will somehow realize that she can only have one accident: "If she has to sit in those wet clothes, she'll think twice about having an accident." If parents offer you this explanation, they probably believe it. You will need to gently explain that this might be quite logical for adults, but two-year-old children don't think (or learn) in that way. This can be maddening to you as caregivers because you know how important it is to keep children clean and dry while they learn to use the toilet.

As our original task force met, we were surprised at the intense feelings many of our members expressed over clothing issues. Caregivers described their frustration at not being taken seriously and their anger when they believed that parents were ignoring their requests for clothing on purpose. More than one person said, "They know they don't have to send in the extra clothes because they know we'll change their kids anyway." Talking about this statement led us to the real heart of the matter. We didn't like the feeling of being taken advantage of, the feeling that parents had us over a barrel, the feeling that parents were getting away with something. We also realized that sometimes we reacted by trying to punish parents in some way. Once we got this out in the open, we were able to think about it more clearly. We had to start by realizing and accepting that, indeed, we could not control whether parents sent in an adequate supply of clothing. From there we realized and accepted that we did not have to base our own actions on what parents did or did not do; our actions could be based on what we decided to do. We found that it really changed our perspective, our feelings, and our actions once we said out loud, "You know, some parents are just not going to send in enough clothes."

When considering possible solutions to this problem, the physical and emotional well-being of children has to come first. We heard of programs that tried to punish parents by sending children home in wet clothes. You simply cannot do this. First, this is uncomfortable, unfair, and possibly humiliating to the child. It certainly doesn't help the child feel comfortable with the new process or confident in his ability to master potty training. There are also health considerations. Urine-soaked or feces-soiled clothes increase the likelihood of infection spreading. Finally, it is mean-spirited and hinders attempts to create partnerships with parents.

Other programs used the extra clothes one child brought for a child who did not have enough. This creates all kinds of problems. Now the first child may not have enough clothes, but the parents think she does because they remember bringing in enough. The parents of the second child might not wash and return the clothes quickly enough. The first child might object very strongly to have her clothes on someone else. She is not refusing to share, she simply sees a situation that is not right and can't understand it.

The most workable solution is to have a supply of "program clothes" to use when children run out of clothing. The program collects clothing in sizes and styles appropriate to toilet learning. These clothes can come from garage sales, thrift stores, or donations from parents in the program whose children have outgrown them. Parents need to know that you will first use the child's own extra clothing and, if those run out, you'll use center clothes. We know that some people feel this rewards the parents who don't send in enough clothes and punishes the ones who do. This can be difficult because no one wants to feel taken advantage of. However, we must realize that we can't force parents to send in clothes; we don't control them. What we *can* do is come up with solutions that meet the needs of the children.

6

Problems for Parents and Caregivers

When Potty Training Doesn't Go According to Plan

When parents and caregivers have worked together to help children learn to use the toilet, they expect the process to go smoothly. However, there is no guarantee that the process will be problem-free. Here are several problem situations our task force members experienced and suggestions for dealing with them.

When Children Just Plain Refuse to Go

Some children refuse to learn to use the toilet. They wet themselves, soil themselves, or try to hold back their bowel movements and become constipated. Many of these children also refuse to sit on the toilet or will use it only if they are taken by parents or caregivers. A child who is over three and has not learned to use the toilet after several months of trying may simply be resistant to the process. More practice at controlling the bladder and bowels is not necessary; their control is already impressive. Often children are resistant because adults remind them too much about going potty, often in the form of lectures and nagging. Even though it may seem logical to adults to try to control the toilet learning process, to the child it can feel like too much pressure. All adults need to realize that pressure is in the eye of the beholder. Parents and caregivers are often surprised that the child feels any kind of pressure because they don't regard what they're doing as "pressure." The child's response can be to simply refuse to cooperate. It may be the only way the child has to assert some kind of control of her own. Adults who are dealing with this situation need to remove the pressure and let the child take responsibility for using the toilet. This may mean that for a time she will continue to be wet or soiled, but when the pressure is off, children usually choose to use the toilet rather than be uncomfortable.

One suggestion to help children feel more of a sense of control is to let them set a timer to indicate when it's time to use the potty. At a meeting of caregivers and parents, a parent reported wonderful results with this technique. She showed her daughter how to set the timer for an hour and told her that when the timer rang, she would know it was time to use the potty. After using the potty, the little girl reset the timer herself. While the timer was actually a substitute for the mother's reminders, the little girl could control setting the timer, which made all the difference.

When a Child Will Use the Potty at Home, but Not at the Program (or Vice Versa)

Children need to feel comfortable to be able to use the toilet. All of us know adults who do not like to use unfamiliar toilets, who can't go if anyone else is nearby, or who will hold it until they get home. If a child will use the toilet in one place but not the other, adults need to find out what the child sees as the difference between the two. It may be a privacy issue, one toilet may not feel as stable or secure as the other one, the child may be worried about having enough time to "get all the poop out," or may feel pressured in some other way. It is important for us to remember that pressure is in the eye of the person experiencing it. Adults need to find ways to change the toileting situation and help the child be comfortable with it. If children are able to talk, parents and caregivers can ask the child directly,

> I know it's hard for you to use the toilet here and that you feel okay about using it at home [or the program, or whatever the child calls the child care situation]. I wonder why. (Note: The "I wonder . . ." approach does not demand an answer from the child, nor does it call for a yes-or-no answer.)

You can also ask, "What could we do about the potty here?" Then you need to listen to what the child says, and see if parents can use the response to make changes in the toileting situation for the child. Adults also need to resist the possible temptation to punish or force the child into using the potty. This only reinforces the child's feeling that this is not a safe place to relax enough to use the toilet.

When Children Will Not Have Bowel Movements in the Potty

When the task force was originally doing its work on potty training issues, Carol Eisenberg, the nurse practitioner who was working with us, talked about children who try to keep from having bowel movements. When children have had painful bowel movements, they may try to keep it from happening again. Usually this involves squeezing the sphincter muscles when they feel the urge to have a bowel movement. Instead of passing the stool, they hold it in. This can lead to serious and painful constipation. She also pointed out that this holding back can also occur when a child feels pressured to use the potty. The child tries to resist the pressure by refusing to let go—holding the stool in. Sometimes children who are trying to hold the stool in develop rituals around having bowel movements. They will go in a particular place (often a private place) or make specific gestures (such as shifting from foot to foot while shaking their hands) or make specific sounds.

When adults notice children using such rituals to have bowel movements, they should treat them as indications of constipation and "holding back." Children who are constipated must see their health care provider so this problem can be treated. Adults should not use laxatives, enemas, or suppositories unless directed to do so by the health care provider. Parents and caregivers need to look carefully at how a child who is (or has been) constipated is responding to the potty training process and see if they need to make changes. They may need to reduce the pressure the child feels even if it doesn't seem like much at all to the adults.

In the years since the task force worked on the original resource, I have spoken with many parents who have experienced this problem with their children. I also experienced it as a parent firsthand and found many similarities in the situations parents described. In almost all cases the children were boys, and in every case the child had actually had several bowel movements in the toilet, and then stopped. The child continued to urinate in the toilet, but was adamant about not having bowel movements in the toilet. Those of us who experienced this were convinced that our children knew when they needed to have their bowel movements and that they carefully and purposefully avoided the potty to do it. We found that they picked an out-of-the-way place and then carefully went to that place every time they had their bowel movements. When we tried to quickly grab them in the act and get them to the potty, their screams were bloodcurdling and filled with sincere fear. It also became clear that the children who did this were overwhelmingly very well-behaved children who were also quite cautious by nature. They were not having accidents and at the same time they were not deliberately trying to do the wrong thing; they were just trying to avoid having bowel movements in the potty. We may not have been sure why they were so fearful, but their reasons must have been very strong indeed if these otherwise cooperative children would rather do the wrong thing than have bowel movements in the potty.

Here is a suggestion that has been successful with children in this situation. Temporarily stop interfering with their bowel movements. When they have had their bowel movements speak to them in a calm and matter-of-fact way, "You had a bowel movement in your pants. Soon you will have your bowel movements in the potty. Let's go to the bathroom and finish up," which sets up the expectation that they will use the potty in the future. (In one case, a mother told her son, "I know you will have your BM in the potty soon." The child responded, "But not today.") Don't scold or yell at the child. These children know they should have used the potty, but they are too worried or scared to do it. Then take the child to the bathroom and continue the toileting process. Put the feces in the potty and wipe the child or have them wipe themselves. Flush the toilet and wash the child's hands or have the child wash his own hands. Many parents I have worked with have reported that this helped the situation and took a good deal of pressure off them and their children.

When Children Want to Play with Their Feces

Adults are often surprised (and then uncomfortable) to find that children may be very interested in their stool. Most children want to look at what they have just produced and many expect adults to be just as interested. Some children may even be quite angry at the suggestion that it needs to be gotten rid of. "What? Flush away this creation? Are you crazy?"

It is not unusual for some children to want to touch the stool or try to play in it. Adults need to remember that children are not born with a distaste for waste products, and most often the child is demonstrating simple curiosity. We can't however, let children handle their stool because it is too unsanitary. As we talk with children, we must explain what we do with the stool instead of what we don't do. Tell children, "When the poop comes out of your body, it goes in the potty. Then we look at it, and then we flush." This needs to be combined with careful supervision during and after using the potty.

When Children Regress

Sometimes children use the toilet successfully and consistently and then begin to wet themselves or have bowel movements in their pants regularly. This is different from the accidents that occur when children forget to go because they're too busy playing or can't get their clothes off fast enough. When children regress it is often because they are not quite emotionally ready for this step or because they are dealing with a stressful situation. For example, they may decide they don't want to be a big boy who uses the potty especially if a new baby comes along and being the big boy has distinct disadvantages.

Adults need to look at what else is going on in the life of a child who regresses when it comes to using the potty. Parents and caregivers need to talk about what may be going on at home or in the program to find out what may be triggering the regression. They must then work together to comfort and reassure the child, try to deal with the situation causing the regression, and continue to expect and encourage the child to use the potty. Here, again, is where the perspective of potty training as a process gradually leading to self-help can serve as a guide. When children regress it may be tempting to decide to call off the potty training. But if you know you're going in the direction of mastery and of self-help, you can withstand taking a few steps backward until you're back on track. Parents and caregivers should be careful not to give in to the temptation to punish the child or browbeat her into getting back on the potty track. Occasionally parents and caregivers suspect that a child is regressing just to see how the adults will respond. The best response is a calm reaction coupled with the expectation, by both parents and caregivers, that the child will use the potty.

When Children Use Potty Training to Control Adults

After a period of time when children have been taken to the potty, because their parents and caregivers realize or think they need to go, the children will begin to ask (or demand) to be taken with urgent cries of "Potty, Mommy," or "Pee-pee, now!" Most parents and caregivers are pleased and so will quickly jump up and take the child to the potty. Now, there is not much children this age can do to get such a quick reaction from adults. Just by saying these few magic words, the child can get an adult's full attention and can make the adult leave almost any situation for a little personal trip to the potty. What a wonderful bit of power this turns out to be. And the child soon figures out that the best part is—you don't even have to really *do* anything on the potty. You just have to *say* that you do, and the adults will have to take you! Almost every child figures this out and milks it to its full advantage.

And almost every adult who has been led on one of these dry potty trips wants to keep the child from using this power. A parent will ask, "How can I get him to stop using potty training as a way to control me?" Adults should try looking at it in a different way. The child is doing this not because he is bad or is on the path to becoming a manipulator, but simply because he has discovered that it works—and works quite well! And any intelligent person will continue doing something that works! Now, why on earth should that child not make full use of this newfound advantage?

One of our task force members had a three-year-old daughter who could always sense when there were about three minutes left in her brother's high school basketball games. With great urgency she announced to her daddy (one of the world's foremost basketball fans), "I hafta go potty."

Despite her father's begging, "Just hold it until the end of the game," she persisted. "I hafta go now, Daddy. I hafta go real bad, Daddy." And daddy took her to the bathroom where she sat on the toilet and calmly announced, "It won't come out."

Adults need to understand that children will ask to go to the potty when they really don't have to as a way to test the control they have over the process and to see if the adults will take them when they say they have to go. Adults don't have to like this aspect of the learning process, but it almost always occurs and is an indication that the child is reasoning, analyzing, and making predictions—all higher-level thinking skills. Since most children stop this on their own, adults should save their sanity by simply taking the child to the potty when he asks to go and not reacting strongly when the child does not actually go.

This issue also helps adults understand how important it is that toileting become a self-help skill. Once the procedure has been set, children should not always have to ask adults to take them to the toilet at home or in the program. They should be able to pull down their own pants, sit on the potty, wipe themselves, flush the toilet, and wash their hands. Children should be encouraged to do as much for themselves as possible. At the same time, they learn that sometimes they will need help from adults because it may not be safe for them to go to the bathroom by themselves or the bathroom may not be set up for young children.

7

Potty Training Policies and Procedures

We recommend that programs think about, develop, and communicate policies about potty training. It may be tempting to roll your eyes and mumble that you can't believe someone is actually suggesting having policies about potty training, of all things! Policies are important because they put you in the position of setting the stage for how potty training will happen in your program.

If you have no policies, you may find yourself reacting to or trying to follow a range of suggestions and requests from parents. Most of us in the early care and education field think of ourselves as offering programs where best practices have been developed and implemented. In this way we are a little like schools.

Parents, however, often see our programs quite differently because most of them pay for child care directly. This makes child care look much more like any other consumer service where the customer is always right. In consumer services, for example, the customers determine how their steaks will be cooked or how much starch should be used in their shirts.

For many parents, then, it may seem perfectly reasonable to give you directions on when and how they want their children potty trained. And while parents are indeed your customers, what is best for children must be your guide. If you have a policy that is built on a perspective such as the one in this book, you will be not only educating parents about potty training, but also letting them know that you have put a great deal of thought into working on this skill with their children.

Written policies that are clear and well-thought-out help all adults involved with the child. These policies must be based on good early childhood practice. They cannot reflect or accommodate the wishes of adults—caregivers or parents—that are based solely on convenience or that violate good early childhood practice. Another reason to have policies and procedures is to ensure that staff have the information and support they need to carry out potty training in a consistent way throughout the program. A child care program without policies may find that potty training ends up being a matter of the personal preferences of the caregivers in the toddler room. Written policies also help to reinforce any statements about potty training that are part of state child care regulations. In New York state, for example, the regulations specifically say that child care programs may not use any potty training methods that "frighten, humiliate, or demean" a child.

During task force meetings, it was very easy to identify things parents did that made potty training difficult for children or for us as caregivers. As we worked on problem areas, it became apparent to us that sometimes our programs had policies or practices that actually encouraged or pressured parents to force potty training on their children without considering readiness.

We identified several such policies and practices that we knew of in our community. We recognized that while many of them might meet our needs as adults, what must guide our decisions about policies and practices is whether and how they support children in developing self-help mastery of potty training. We must also consider their effect on parents. Considering these policies and practices forced us to take a good, hard look at how our programs really deal with individual differences. The marketing literature from almost all early childhood programs contains statements about acceptance of and attention to individual children's needs and development. We must make sure our policies and practices support these statements.

The following program practices and policies contradict good developmental practice for potty training:

- **Having all children begin potty training at the same time or whenever they move into a specific room.**
  All children develop differently and will be ready to begin the toilet learning process at different ages.

- **Charging higher fees for children who are not potty trained than for children in the same room who are use the potty and do not need to have diapers changed.**
  This encourages parents to ask or insist that their children be potty trained so they can pay a lower fee. It also raises problems about whether a child is really potty trained or not. A parent may insist the child use the potty, put the child in underwear, and then be angry with the child for having accidents. While it may be more work to care for children in diapers, programs do not charge more for children who need more attention than others, who eat more than others, or who use more art materials than others.

- **Using potty training as a sole gatekeeper for moving the child up to an advanced group.**
  We should not hold children back from their peer group based on any one skill. Many caregivers in preschool rooms argue

that they don't have time to deal with children who still have accidents. Early childhood professionals must be willing and able to help children who are still in the process of learning to use the toilet. The average age for children to be potty trained in the United States is twenty-seven months, with a range of up to three to four years old. (Behrman et al. 2000). It is therefore pretty likely that some children in preschool rooms will still need help with potty training.

A useful, effective policy should include the following:

- A statement of the program's potty training philosophy or practice
- Ways parents and caregivers will work together to coordinate the potty training process between home and the program
- Age when the program will consider beginning the potty training process with a child
- Reasons for stopping the process for a time
- Techniques the program uses with accidents
- Procedures, routines, strategies, and techniques the program will and will *not* use

Sample Potty Training Policy

At our program we base our potty training practices on the following philosophy:

- Learning to use the toilet is an important self-help skill for toddlers.
- We consider potty training to be a process that will help children gradually master toileting as a self-help skill. We want potty training at our program to be a nonstressful experience that is appropriate to each child's individual development and involves the child, parents, and caregivers. We believe that when children are in group care, parents and caregivers must work as partners so children can be comfortable, confident, and successful while they learn toileting skills.

We will take the following steps to support the best possible potty training experience for you and your child.

- We will work with parents to ensure that toilet training is consistent between home and our program. We will use written material and conferences before a child actually begins the process. Parents and caregivers will maintain communication about progress and will share any concerns or questions they have.

- We will consider beginning the potty training process when there are indications that a child is ready. Our program has a set of readiness questions that both caregivers and parents use to tell when a child is ready to begin potty training. We don't begin the process for other reasons (such as expense of diapers, convenience, age of child, comparison to other children, among others) if the indications show that the child is not ready.
- We will never force a child to sit on the potty. Under no circumstance will a child be tied or strapped to a potty.
- We don't bribe children to use the potty. We cannot cooperate with parents' attempts to promise children treats or rewards if they use the potty.
- We will not punish or shame children in any way for accidents. We recognize that accidents are part of the learning process and may be attributed to many factors. Children will never be forced to clean up the mess because they made it.
- We will not allow children to remain in wet or soiled clothing following accidents. We will change them immediately into dry clothing. This demonstrates respect for the child, acceptance of accidents as inevitable, and understanding that young children do not learn by intimidation, fear, or shame. We will need an adequate supply of clothes during the toilet training process to keep the child dry all day, and we will give parents clothing guidelines.
- We will not agree to practices that violate state regulations about potty training or that conflict with our philosophy and potty training practice.

References

American Academy of Pediatrics. 1998. *Toilet training.* Elk Grove Village, Ill.: American Academy of Pediatrics.

Behrman, R. E., R. M. Kliegman, H. B. Jenson, eds. 2000. *Nelson textbook of pediatrics.* 16th ed. Philadelphia: W. B. Saunders Co.

Brazelton, T. B., E. R. Christophersen, A. C. Frauman, P. A. Gorski, J. M. Poole, A. C. Stadtler, and C. L. Wright. 1999. Instruction, timeliness, and medical influences affecting toilet training. *Pediatrics* 103 (June) 1353–58.

Gray, Carol, and A. L. White. 2002. *My social stories book.* London: Jessica Kingsley Publishers Ltd.

Schum, T. R., T. M. Kolb, T. M. McAuliffe, M. D. Simms, R. L. Underhill, and M. Lewis. 2002. Sequential acquisition of toilet training skills: A descriptive study of gender and age differences in normal children. *Pediatrics* 109 (3): e48.

Resources

You may wish to have other resources to consult about potty training and to suggest to parents. You won't have any trouble finding such books and resources. Many are wonderful and very useful. Others, however, are not. Books that claim to have a simple, one-size-fits-all, foolproof method of potty training, that promise children will be potty trained in one day, or insist that there is a specific piece of equipment that will guarantee success are good ones to avoid. If there was one foolproof method of potty training, if there was a way to guarantee children could be potty trained in a day, if there was a magic piece of equipment, wouldn't everyone be using it? Potty training would no longer be an issue for parents or for child care programs and providers. We could just have National All-Toddlers-Stay-Home-Today-and-Get-Potty-Trained-and-Be-Done-with-It Day.

I suggest books and resources that are consistent with the perspective of this book. Here are several excellent resources for you and for parents:

The American Academy of Pediatrics Guide to Toilet Training, by the American Academy of Pediatrics. 2003. New York: Random House.

This resource is a comprehensive potty training guide for families. It recognizes that not all children are ready for potty training at the same time, and that not all children respond to the same approach. The advice is from some of the nation's finest pediatricians. It answers parents' frequently asked questions and contains information and specific tips for toilet training girls, boys, twins, and children with special needs. This would be a great resource to have on hand for parents to use.

You Can Go to the Potty, by William Sears, M.D., Martha Sears, R.N., and Christie Watts Kelly. Illustrated by Renée Andriani. 2002. New York: Little, Brown and Company.

This book is part of the Sears Children's Library. Written for adults and children, it starts with very useful notes for parents and caregivers and puts potty training in a developmental context. The section for children addresses them directly rather than telling the story of potty training from another child's perspective. One of the best features of the book is a series of "answers for the very curious," responses to real questions children are likely to ask and great, simple answers adults can give them.

Parents and caregivers of children with Autistic Spectrum Disorders (ASD) need resources specifically designed to help them. One strategy to help children with ASD is using a "social story." Social stories "describe what most of us dismiss as obvious, patiently considering the world through the eyes of a child with ASD. A Social Story can inform, reassure, instruct, console, support, praise, and correct children with ASD *and* those who work on their behalf" (Gray and White 2002). Social stories are an approach developed by Carol Gray who writes and lectures on the subject. Information is available on her Web site, www.thegraycenter.org. *My Social Stories Book,* edited by Carol Gray and Abbie Leigh White (Jessica Kingsley Publishers 2002), contains a collection of social stories including several on potty training.

Potty Training Books for Children

One way parents and programs can build on a child's interest in learning to use the toilet is through books that show children learning this skill. Have these books available for adults to share with children or for children to "read" themselves.

Caillou: Potty Time, by Joceline Sanschagrin. 1987. Montreal: Chouette Publishing.

This board book with simple, colorful pictures is one of the five books in this Canadian series about Caillou, a toddler who is learning new skills. Here he learns to use the potty.

My Big Girl Potty and *My Big Boy Potty,* by Joanna Cole. Illustrated by Maxie Chambliss. 2000. New York: HarperCollins Publishing.

Child characters explain toileting—how you have to sit a long time on the potty and nothing might even happen. They talk about the whole process of using the potty including wiping and hand washing. The books have good potty training hints for parents.

My Potty and I: A Friend in Need (Berenstain Bears Baby Board Books), by Stan and Jan Berenstain. 1999. New York: Random House.

This board book, with baby bear versions of the familiar Berenstain Bears, has text with simple rhymes. The story is mostly about knowing when to go to the potty and the problem of accidents.

My Potty Book for Boys and *My Potty Book for Girls.* 2001. New York: Dorling Kindersley Publishing, Inc.

These board books have photographs of real children from different racial and ethnic groups. The children at the end of the book (the end of the potty training process) are obviously older and bigger than the children at the beginning of the book.

Once Upon a Potty, by Alana Frankel. 1979. New York: HarperFestival.

This classic book was written and illustrated by the author for her own children. Available in two editions—one book for boys and one for girls—this is the story of a child making the transition from diapers to the potty. Various mishaps in the potty training process are also covered. The mother plays an important role in this book.

The Potty Book for Girls and *The Potty Book for Boys,* by Alyssa Satin Capucilli. Illustrated by Dorothy Stott. 2000. Hauppauge, New York: Barron's.

The book for girls features Hannah and the book for boys features Henry, who each talk in a rhyming format about what they are able to do for themselves, including getting a potty and learning to use it as another self-help skill.

Uh Oh! Gotta Go! Potty Tales from Toddlers, by Bob McGrath. Illustrated by Shelley Dieterichs. 1996. Hauppauge, New York: Barron's.

Uh Oh! Gotta Go! contains twenty-seven vignettes, each one page long, showing many different toddlers' experiences during the toilet training process. The situations depicted are very true to life and presented in a humorous way using very little text. The illustrations are especially appropriate because they feature children from many racial and ethnic groups. One of the nicest features of this book is the page at the end with a place for the child's photograph. This is one of my favorite books.

What to Expect When You Use the Potty, by Heidi Murkhoff. Illustrated by Laura Rader. 2000. New York: HarperFestival.

Part of the children's series by the coauthor of *What to Expect When You're Expecting,* this books features a question-and-answer format—toddlers supply the questions and Angus, the answer dog, gives the answers. The questions range from the obvious, "Where do pee and poop come from?" to "What if I have to go when I'm not at home?" I like this book because it has answers to questions toddlers may not be able to ask themselves. One thing I do not like in the book is the "potty points" chart shown on one page. The chart, however, is not the focus of the page. This is another of my favorite books.

Appendix

Readiness Questions for Adults

1. **Is your child at least eighteen months old?**

   Children develop the muscles and bladder capacity to begin the potty training process between the ages of eighteen and twenty-four months. It is at least useless and possibly harmful to expect any child to do something that she is physically unable to do.

2. **Are your child's diapers dry for at least two hours at a time?**

   Dry diapers indicate that your child's bladder is large enough and mature enough for potty training to be successful.

3. **Does your child know—and let you know—when he is wet or has a bowel movement?**

   Your child will not be able to successfully learn to use the toilet if he is not even aware of being wet or having had a bowel movement.

4. **Does your child tell you or indicate that she is uncomfortable in wet or soiled diapers?**

   If your child feels quite comfortable with wet or soiled diapers, it will be hard to convince her to urinate and have bowel movements in the potty. A child who is ready to begin the potty training process will pull or tug at wet or soiled diapers or may indicate in another way that she is uncomfortable and wants to be changed.

5. **Can your child sit upright for five minutes?**

   If your child is not able to sit anywhere for five minutes, he won't be able to sit on the potty long enough to urinate and have bowel movements—especially at first.

6. **Can your child undress enough to sit on the potty?**

   Your child needs to be able to do as much of the process independently as possible. She needs to be able to pull down her own pants so that toileting can become a self-help skill. It will be very hard for your child to get to the potty in time if she always has to wait for help with clothing from an adult.

7. **Is your child able to get himself to the potty?**

   For toileting to be a self-help skill, the child needs to be able to take himself to the potty without help from an adult. If your child is already walking, he needs to be able to walk without assistance from adults and without holding onto furniture or the walls.

8. **Does your child follow simple directions?**

   Your child will need to be able to follow directions and cooper-ate with you during this process. She needs to be able and will-ing (most of the time) to follow simple, one-step directions.

9. **Does your child answer simple yes-and-no questions?**

   You want your child to be able to communicate with you and his caregivers during this process, to be able to answer when adults ask if he is wet, ready to use the toilet, and so on.

10. **Does your child imitate others—parents, caregivers, or other children?**

    If your child imitates others (for example, pretending to drink coffee like you do), she will likely imitate others when it comes to potty training too. This is a good thing!

11. **Does your child trust the adults who care for him and feel comfortable with them?**

    Your child will have a difficult time learning this new skill if he doesn't trust the adults who are caring for him.

12. **Does your child show pride, joy, or excitement when she learns new skills?**

    If your child shows pride, joy, or excitement in learning other new skills, that's the way she will approach potty training too. A child who does not seem interested in accomplishing new tasks and mastering new skills may have trouble with potty training.

And finally, some questions for you about yourself!

1. **Do you know what you will have to do to help your child learn to use the potty?**

   You need to know what to expect during the potty training process so you can help your child and make sure that he is successful at potty training.

2. **Are you willing and able to devote the time and attention to helping your child learn to use the potty?**

   You are going to have to make some changes in your routines, some sacrifices, and some time adjustments in order for the potty training process to go smoothly for your child. There will be many times when you will want to say, "Oh, just put her in a diaper for now because . . . " Going back and forth between

being expected to use the potty and being put into diapers—
cloth, disposable, or the pull-up type—is very confusing to
your child. You'll have to consider potty training when you are
making plans for activities. This is inconvenient, but it does
not last long!

Dear Parents,

You are looking forward to having your child learn to use the toilet. You probably feel that you just can't wait for your child to be out of diapers and using the toilet all by herself. At our program we look at potty training as a skill your child will learn gradually. At first children in our program need lots of help and gradually they are able to do more and more themselves. This is our goal: your child will be able to handle toileting all by herself. This means that your child will be actively participating in potty training; we won't be doing everything for her. This is usually a pretty good fit for toddlers because they want to be independent and are trying to do more and more for themselves. We hear them loud and clear, "Me do it!" We want your child to be successful at potty training, so we pay attention to making sure she is ready—that all systems are go—and that all of us are ready to support her.

So, when do we start and what do we do? We use a list of questions that will help us know when your child has the physical development, the understanding, and the motivation to start learning to use the toilet. We would like to look at the list with you and then discuss your ideas about potty training and share our ideas and practices with you.

We want to work together on this because your child will be learning to use the toilet both at home and at our program. Children can't succeed if the expectations and practices change from place to place and adult to adult.

Please let us know when you are ready to consider potty training for your child. If we notice signs that she may be ready, we may contact you first. Either way, we'll work together so she can master this important skill.

Sincerely,

Dear Parents,

Now that your child will be learning to use the potty, you want to make sure that he has clothes that make this process as easy as possible for him. Especially at the beginning, the time between when your child realizes that he needs to urinate and when he actually does it will be very, very short. He won't have to time to struggle with his clothes. It will be discouraging for him to realize he needs to use the toilet and then wet the floor because he couldn't get his clothes off fast enough. As you know, we look at potty training as an important self-help skill for toddlers. Being able to get his own clothes off and on so he can go when he needs to go, all by himself, is very important. Potty training can't become a self-help skill if he can only accomplish it when an adult is available to undo buttons, snaps, and buckles.

We have included a list of clothes to help your child during potty training. We've also included a list of clothes that could make things very difficult. These lists are from parents and teachers with years of potty training experience, who want to share what they've learned with you. Unfortunately, some of these clothes—often the cutest toddler clothes on the market—are the very ones that give toddlers the most trouble when they're learning to use the potty. It is so important for your child to have clothing that he can manage by himself that it is worth using such outfits only on special occasions or putting them away until he can undo all the snaps, buttons, or buckles.

As your child begins learning to use the toilet, we recommend thickly padded training pants. As he experiences success, you can switch to thinner underwear with plastic pants and then to thinner underwear by itself.

We will change your child whenever he is wet or has a bowel movement. We will never allow him to remain in wet or soiled clothes. This means we will be doing a lot of changing at the beginning of the process, which means he will need a lot of extra clothes. We will need at least five pairs of training pants, three pairs of socks, three pairs of pants, and extra shoes available at all times.

If your child runs out of clothes, we will use extra clothing we keep here for this purpose. It is important that you wash and return the clothing. We won't use your child's clothing for other children, and we won't use other children's clothing for your child. It may be tempting to think that if your child only has one set of clean clothes, he will realize that he can't have any accidents and so will be sure not to wet himself. This may seem logical, but only to adults. Young children don't think in those terms. They learn by trial and error (and there will be lots of errors) and by experiencing success.

When your child wets or has a bowel movement in his clothing, we will put it in a plastic bag without rinsing it out. This often surprises parents, and we know that it would be much more convenient for you to get clothing that has been rinsed out. However, we are following recommended standards for infection control which specify that child care centers not rinse out clothing after children urinate, have bowel movements, or vomit in them.

We know this may seem like a lot of extra work, but it is only for a short time, and the rewards for you and your child will be well worth the extra work.

Yours,

Clothing that will help children master potty training

● **Elastic-waist, loose-fitting pants**
We recommend these pants over those with buttons or snaps because they are easy for children to pull up and down themselves.

● **Waist-length undershirts**
Longer undershirts interfere with the toileting process.

● **Thickly padded cotton training pants**
Use thickly padded training pants when potty training starts. They absorb better when children have accidents, and children can pull them up and down themselves.

● **Regular underwear**
As children experience success, allow them to wear underwear. Children can easily pull the underwear up and down themselves; they also give immediate feedback when children have accidents. Underwear must not be a reward for learning to use the potty. It should be considered one of the tools.

● **Lots of extra clothes including training pants, extra pants, socks, and shoes**
We want to be able to clean children up as quickly as possible and with as little fuss as possible. Children must never be forced to stay in clothes that are wet or have a bowel movement in them.

Clothing that makes potty training difficult for children

● **Bib overalls or pants with belts, buckles, snaps, or buttons**
Many toddlers may not have the fine-motor skills or the finger strength to unfasten these on their own.

● **Tight-fitting pants**
Many toddlers may not have the strength, patience, or coordination to pull them down. If they get wet, many adults may not have the strength, patience, or coordination to pull them off.

● **One-piece outfits and jumpsuits**
One-piece outfits require a lot of time to get off. Some of the jump suits that snap in the crotch, but not all the way down the legs, are especially difficult to get out of. These outfits also leave you practically naked just to pee!

● **Onesie-type undershirts or bodysuits**
Many toddlers cannot unsnap these shirts. In addition, the long backs frequently fall in the toilet and get wet. Children may feel that they have failed because their clothes got wet even though they got all the urine in the potty.

● **Dresses, skirts, and tights**
Toileting can be difficult when little girls try to use one hand to hold the dress or skirt up and have only one hand available to pull down panties. Tights are usually difficult to pull down and seem especially difficult to pull back up. Skirts can work if they can be pulled up and down easily like slacks.

● **Pull-up type disposable diapers**
Disposable, pull-up type diapers are marketed as a type of underwear that is especially good for potty training. They may be designed to look like underwear but they function like a diaper, making it very hard for toddlers to feel when they are wet. Toddlers then have a difficult time making the connection between the feeling of a full bladder and the need to use the potty.

Other Resources from Redleaf Press

No Biting: Policy and Practice for Toddler Programs
Gretchen Kinnell for the Child Care Council of Onondaga County, Inc.
The "how-to" manual for every toddler program seeking to address biting incidents from developmental, emotional, and practical perspectives.

Prime Times: A Handbook for Excellence in Infant and Toddler Programs
Jim Greenman and Anne Stonehouse
An essential guide to establishing a high-quality program for infants and toddlers.

Infant and Toddler Experiences
Fran Hast and Ann Hollyfield
Filled with experiences—not activities—that promote the healthiest development in infants and toddlers.

More Infant and Toddler Experiences
Fran Hast and Ann Hollyfield
Filled with over 100 engaging new ways to fill infants' and toddlers' lives with rich experiences that reflect and celebrate each child's development.

Quick Quality Check for Infant and Toddler Programs
Michelle Knoll and Marion O'Brien
Quick Quality Check for Infant and Toddler Programs is a quick, practical, and easy-to-use method for monitoring and evaluating the quality and consistency of care provided in infant and toddler programs. Designed for center and program directors.

Beginning with Babies
Mary Lou Kinney and Patricia Witt Ahrens
An easy-to-use guide containing dozens of activities to help teachers provide developmentally appropriate care for children from birth through fifteen months.

Practical Solutions to Practically Every Problem: The Early Childhood Teacher's Manual, Revised Edition
Steffen Saifer
Find solutions quickly and easily! This updated classic offers hundreds of tested solutions for the tricky problems, questions, and concerns that are part of every early childhood teacher's day.

800-423-8309
www.redleafpress.org